EXPERIMENTS WITH WEATHER

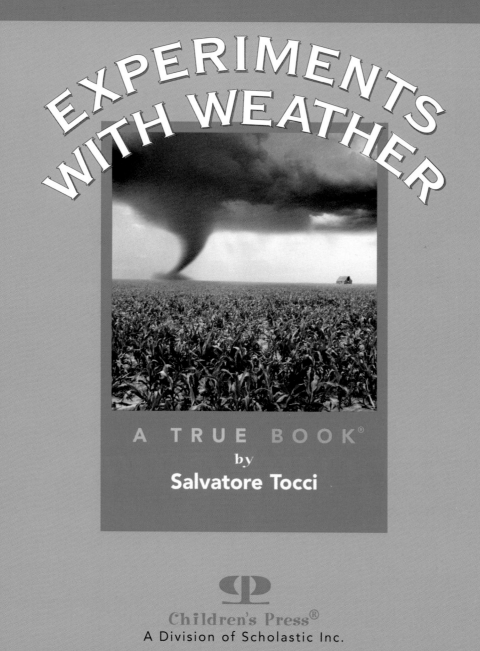

A T R U E   B O O K®

by

Salvatore Tocci

Children's Press®
A Division of Scholastic Inc.

New York Toronto London Auckland Sydney
Mexico City New Delhi Hong Kong
Danbury, Connecticut

According to a popular legend, groundhogs can predict the length of winter.

Reading Consultant
Susan Virgilio

Science Consultant
Tenley Andrews

The photo on the cover shows a lightning storm. The photo on the title page shows a tornado in a cornfield.

The author and publisher are not responsible for injuries or accidents that occur during or from any experiments. Experiments should be conducted in the presence of or with the help of an adult. Any instructions of the experiments that require the use of sharp, hot, or other unsafe items should be conducted by or with the help of an adult.

Library of Congress Cataloging-in-Publication Data
Tocci, Salvatore.
   Experiments with weather / by Salvatore Tocci.
     p. cm. (A true book)
Includes bibliographical references and index.
Contents: Will Phil see his shadow? — What is the weather? — Experiment 1, Taking up space — Experiment 2, Rising up — Experiment 3, Expanding and cooling — Can you feel the breeze? — Experiment 4, Heating the air — Experiment 5, Blowing in the wind — Experiment 6, Checking the humidity — Is a storm coming? — Experiment 7, Checking the pressure — Experiment 8, Making clouds — Experiment 9, Creating sparks — Fun with weather — Experiment 10, Swirling around.
   ISBN 0-516-22790-4 (lib. bdg.)   0-516-27809-6 (pbk.)
   1. Meteorology—Experiments—Juvenile literature. [1. Weather—Experiments. 2. Experiments.] I. Title. II. Series.
QC863.5 .T63 2003
551.5'078—dc21

2002015260

CHILDREN'S PRESS, and A TRUE BOOK®, and associated logos are trademarks and or registered trademarks of Scholastic Library Publishing. SCHOLASTIC and associated logos are trademarks and or registered trademarks of Scholastic Inc.
1 2 3 4 5 6 7 8 9 10 R 12 11 10 09 08 07 06 05 04 03

Contents

Will Phil See His Shadow?

Have you ever heard of Punxsutawney Phil? Although you may never have heard of him, Phil is very famous. Every year on February 2, people gather in a little town in Pennsylvania called Punxsutawney. They wait for Phil to come out of his home.

Phil is not a person. He is a groundhog, which is a small animal that lives underground. According to legend, if Phil comes out of his hole and sees his shadow, there will be another six weeks of winter. If he does not see his shadow, spring will arrive early. This legend has become so popular that February 2 is known throughout the United States as Groundhog Day.

Forecasting the weather based on what Phil sees is not

scientific. However, weather forecasting is actually very scientific. For example, satellites in orbit continuously transmit information about weather conditions. Planes fly into hurricanes to obtain information that scientists use to determine where the storm is likely to head. Fortunately, you do not need a satellite or plane to learn more about the weather. All you need to do is perform the experiments in this book.

What Is the Weather?

Earth's weather takes place within 7 miles (11 kilometers) of its surface. This region above Earth's surface is known as the **atmosphere**. Weather is a description of the conditions that exist in the atmosphere.

Looking up at the sky can give you the impression that the only things you can find in

These weather conditions can be described as a warm day with mostly sunny skies.

the atmosphere are clouds. But the atmosphere is actually filled with invisible gases, such as oxygen and carbon dioxide. This mixture of gases is called air. Is there some way to prove that there is really something in air, even though you cannot see it?

Taking Up Space

Fill the bowl about halfway with water. Place the cork on the water. Hold the glass upside down over th cork. Slowly push the glass down into the water. What happens to the cork?

The water and cork inside the glass are forced down below the level of the water in the bowl. If the glass were really empty, the water and cork inside the glass would be at the same level as the water in the bowl. Although it looks empty, the glass is actually filled with air. This air takes up space and prevents the water in the bowl from filling the glass.

The air inside the glass will keep the water in the bowl from filling the glass.

The sun has a tremendous influence on our weather.

The air in the atmosphere is warmed by the sun, which causes hot summer days. What else happens as air is warmed by the sun?

Experiment 2

Rising Up

You will need:
- pencil
- tissue paper
- scissors
- ruler
- thread
- transparent tape
- lamp

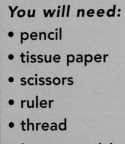

Carefully draw a spiral pattern on the tissue paper. Cut along the line. Next cut a 6-inch (15-centimeter) piece of thread. Tape one end of the thread to the center of the paper spiral. Remove the lamp shade and turn on the light. Hold the free end of the thread so that the paper spiral is about 3 in. (7.5 cm) above the lightbulb. Watch what happens to the paper spiral after a few minutes.

Heat from the light-bulb warms the air above it. As the air gets warmer, it rises. Cooler air moves downward to take the place of the warmer, rising air. This movement of air causes the paper spiral to twirl. As long as the light is on, the heat will continue to make the air above it rise.

The air near the ground may be warm. However, the air near the top of mountains may be cold enough for snow to cover their peaks.

Heat from the sun warms the air in Earth's atmosphere, causing it to rise. If warm air rises, why is the weather always cooler at the top of a mountain?

Experiment 3

Expanding and Cooling

You will need:
- marker
- ruler
- empty plastic milk container with lid
- adult helper
- small pot or kettle
- stove
- oven mitt
- hot plate

Draw a line on the milk container about 1 inch (2.5 cm) from the bottom. Ask an adult to boil some water and then carefully pour it into the container, up to the line. Have the adult put on the oven mitt and cover the container. Then ask the adult to quickly shake the container a few times and place it on the hot plate. Watch what happens to the container.

The hot water warms the air inside the container. When air is warmed, it not only rises, but also expands, or spreads out. As the warm air inside the container expands, it pushes against the sides. This expanding air causes the container to swell up like a barrel.

When air is heated by the sun, it rises and starts to expand. As the air spreads out, it also begins to cool. The air continues to expand and cool as it rises up a mountain. By the time it reaches the top, the air has expanded and cooled quite a bit since it rose from the ground. This is why the weather is always cooler at the top of a mountain.

Can You Feel the Breeze?

If you have ever sat on a beach during the summer, you have probably felt a breeze blowing in from the water. This sea breeze is caused by air that moves from the water toward the land. What causes a sea breeze that can keep you cool on a hot summer day?

Experiment 4

💡

Heating the Air

You will need:
- ruler
- marker
- two large glasses
- dirt
- two thermometers
- table
- desk lamp
- clock
- paper
- pencil

Draw a line 2 in. (5 cm) from the bottom of each glass. Pour water into one glass up to the line. Pour dirt into the second glass up to the line. Place a thermometer in each glass.

Place the glasses on the table near the lamp. After thirty minutes, write down the temperatures of the dirt and water.

Make sure that the two glasses are the same distance from the lamp.

Turn on the lamp. Record the temperature on each thermometer every fifteen minutes for one hour. Then turn off the lamp. Again record the temperatures every fifteen minutes for one hour. Compare how the temperatures of the dirt and water changed each time.

You should find that when the light is on, the temperature of the dirt rises faster than the temperature of the water.

The difference in time it takes for water and land to change temperature creates both sea and land breezes.

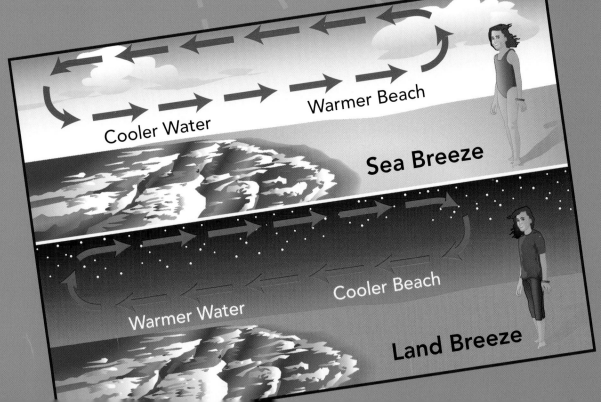

Cooler Water

Warmer Beach

Sea Breeze

Warmer Water

Cooler Beach

Land Breeze

After the lamp is turned off, the temperature of the dirt drops faster than the temperature of the water. Land, such as a beach, heats up faster than a large body of water, such as an ocean, does. The warmer air over land rises and is replaced by the cooler air from over water. This creates a sea breeze during the day. At night, the beach cools faster than the ocean. This creates a land breeze at night.

When the air moves slowly, you feel a breeze. If the air begins to move more quickly, you feel the wind. How can you measure how fast the air is moving?

Blowing in the Wind

Draw two rectangles on the cardboard. Each rectangle should measure 2 in. (5 cm) wide and 12 in. (30 cm) long. Cut out both rectangles. Cross the cardboard strips to make a plus (+) sign and staple them together. Use the ruler to draw two lines, one each from opposite corners where the two strips cross each other to the opposite corners. The point where these two lines cross is the center of the plus sign made by the strips.

Use the marker to color the outside of one of the paper cups. Staple the cups to the ends of the cardboard strips. Make sure that all the cups face the same direction. Push the pin through the center of the strips and into the eraser. Take everything outside. Place a small lump of modeling clay on a flat surface, such as a tree stump, fence rail, or the top step of a ladder. Stick the sharpened point of the pencil into the clay so that it stands up straight.

23

As the wind blows, count the number of times the colored cup spins past you in one minute. Have your helper keep track of the time. The instrument you have made to measure wind speed is called an **anemometer**. Your anemometer measures wind speed in revolutions (spins) per minute. Try measuring wind speed at different locations and during different times of the day. How do your wind speeds compare?

Weather forecasters use anemometers that measure wind speed in miles per hour or kilometers per hour. They also use a device that measures how much moisture, or **humidity**, is in the air. Humidity is reported as a percentage. For example, the humidity on a muggy summer day may be 90 percent. This means that the air is holding 90 percent of all the moisture it can. Learn how you can use two thermometers to tell if the humidity is low or high.

25

Experiment 6

Checking the Humidity

Wet the cotton ball with water and place it over the bulb of one of the thermometers. Place both thermometers on the table. Set the fan so that it will blow on the bulbs of both thermometers. Turn on the fan. After ten minutes, turn off the fan. Record the temperatures on both thermometers. Do this experiment twice, once on a cool, sunny day and again on a rainy day.

The thermometer that was covered with the moist cotton ball should show a lower

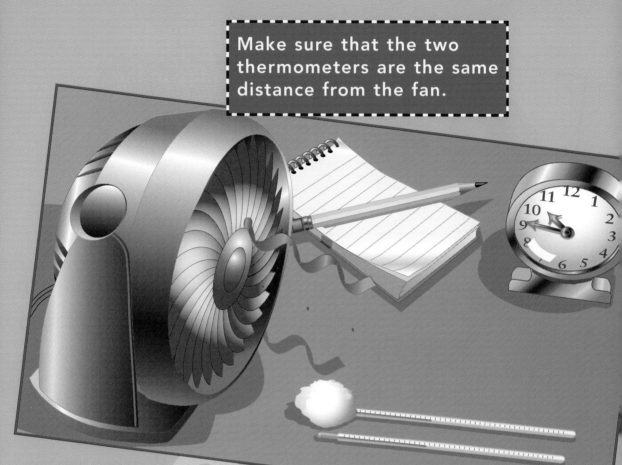

Make sure that the two thermometers are the same distance from the fan.

temperature.
Subtract the temperature reading on this thermometer from the reading on the other thermometer. How does the difference between the two readings you get on a sunny day compare with the difference you get on a rainy day?

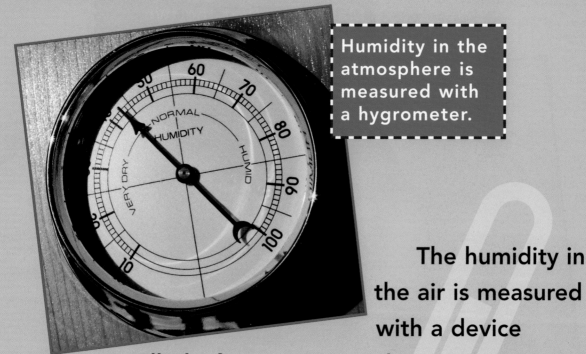

The humidity in the air is measured with a device called a **hygrometer**. A hygrometer contains two thermometers. One is called a dry bulb thermometer, which is just a regular thermometer. The other one is called a wet bulb thermometer.

Your wet bulb thermometer cools as water evaporates from the cotton ball. The faster the water evaporates, the lower the temperature gets on this thermometer. Cool, sunny days usually have low humidity, which means that the air is dry. On these days, the water on the cotton ball evaporates quickly and cools the thermometer. As a result, there is a large drop in the temperature. You should see a large difference in the temperature readings between the two thermometers on days with low humidity.

The difference in temperature readings between these two thermometers is 25 degrees. This large difference indicates low humidity.

The difference in temperature readings between these two thermometers is 5 degrees. This small difference indicates high humidity.

Rainy days have high humidity, which means that the air holds a lot of moisture. On these days, the water on the cotton ball evaporates slowly, and there will be less of a drop in temperature. You should see a smaller difference in the temperature readings between the two thermometers on days with high humidity. If the humidity is very high, a storm may be coming.

Is a Storm Coming?

Weather forecasters often report the barometric pressure and tell whether it is rising or falling. A **barometer** is an instrument that measures **air pressure**. The gases in the air are always moving and bouncing into objects. When they bounce into something, such as your skin, they push or press against it. This creates air pressure.

31

You do not feel the air pressure pushing in on you because the air inside you is pushing out with the same force. In this case, the air pressure inside your body equals the air pressure outside your body. See how you can tell when the air pressure around you is changing.

Experiment 7

Checking the Pressure

You will need:
- plastic wrap
- empty coffee can
- rubber band
- straight pin
- straw
- tape
- ruler
- thermometer
- table
- pencil
- paper

Stretch the plastic wrap over the top of the can. Hold the wrap in place with a rubber band. Push the pin through the end of the straw. Place the straw on the plastic wrap so that about one-third of it sticks out past the edge of the can. Tape the straw to the can. Stand the ruler and thermometer upright and tape them to a wall. Place the can on the table so that the pin points to the ruler.

Record the number on the ruler at which the needle is pointing. Also record the temperature and the weather conditions.

Check your
barometer
several times
a day for a
week. Make
sure to take your read-
ings on the ruler only if the temperature is
the same as it was when you set up your barometer. This way, the only thing that can cause the
needle to move is a change in air pressure (and
not a change in temperature). In what kind of
weather does your barometer rise? What does a
falling barometer indicate about the weather?

On a rainy day, a rising barometer indicates that fair weather is on the way. On a sunny day, a falling barometer indicates that the air pressure is dropping. Low barometric pressure is a sign that a storm is approaching. Perhaps a storm never developed when you were taking your barometer readings. If not, here's your chance to make your own stormy weather.

Experiment 8

💡

Making Clouds

You will need:
- measuring cup
- large clear plastic bottle with cap
- table
- adult helper
- match

Pour one-third cup of warm water into the bottle. Cap the bottle tightly. Shake the bottle for thirty seconds and then place it on the table. Squeeze and then release the bottle several times. Remove the cap. Ask an adult to light a match and hold it over the mouth of the bottle. Quickly squeeze the bottle to put out the match. Then slowly release the bottle so that the smoke is drawn into the bottle. Quickly replace the cap and tighten it. Watch what happens inside the bottle.

A cloud forms inside the bottle. This cloud is formed by tiny water droplets that cling to the particles of smoke from the match.

The cloud that forms inside the bottle will last for only a few seconds. Darken the room and use a flashlight to see it better.

A cloud in the sky is made of billions of tiny water droplets that cling to very tiny salt particles that have traveled high into the air. These water droplets slowly clump together. Eventually, they get large enough to fall to Earth as raindrops. A storm may not only bring rain, but also lightning.

Experiment 9

Creating Sparks

You will need:
- pushpin
- aluminum pie pan
- pencil with eraser
- foam plate or tray
- table
- piece of wool

Carefully push the pin through the center of the aluminum pan from the bottom. Push the eraser into the pin. Place the foam plate upside down on the table. Rub the bottom of the plate fast and hard with the wool. Pick up the aluminum pan, using the pencil as a handle. Place the pan on top of the plate. Darken the room. Touch the aluminum pan with your finger. You should see tiny sparks jump between the pan and your finger. These tiny sparks are just like the huge sparks of lightning that jump between the clouds and Earth during a storm.

If you do not see any sparks, try rubbing the foam plate with the wool again.

Fun With Weather

Instruments, like hygrometers and barometers, provide information used to forecast the weather. This information can help people prepare for snowstorms or hurricanes. Unfortunately, there is no way to prepare for a tornado because it forms too quickly to

predict. As a result, tornadoes can cause a lot of damage. Fortunately, you can create a tornado that does no damage at all.

Swirling Around

You will need:
- two 1-liter plastic soda bottles
- food coloring
- masking tape
- table

Fill one bottle about three-fourths full with water. Add several drops of food coloring and mix by gently swirling the bottle. Place the empty bottle over the bottle that contains water. Tape the mouths of the two bottles together. Turn the bottles over so that the one with water in it is on top. Hold the bottles by their mouths and immediately swirl them for about five seconds. Place the bottles on the table. As the water drains from the top bottle, it should form a spinning whirlpool.

A tornado forms
when the air spins very rapidly,
like the water in the bottle.

To Find Out More

If you would like to learn more about weather, check out these additional resources.

 **Books**

Allaby, Michael. **How the Weather Works.** Reader's Digest Adult, 1999.

Ardley, Neil. **The Science Book of Weather.** Gulliver Books, 1992.

Breen, Mark and Kathleen Friestad. **The Kid's Book of Weather Forecasting.** Williamson Publishing, 2000.

Gardner, Robert and David Webster. **Science Projects about Weather.** Enslow Publishers, 1994.

Haslam, Andrew and Barbara Taylor. **Weather (Make It Work!).** Two-Can Publishers, 2000.

Kerrod, Robin. **Weather.** Gareth Stevens, 1998.

VanCleave, Janice. **Weather.** John Wiley & Sons, 1995.

Organizations and Online Sites

Internet Weather Links
http://www.uen.org/utahlink/weather/link2.html

You can use this site to access others, including ones that are resources for weather experiments and cloud identification.

National Oceanic and Atmospheric Administration (NOAA)
http://www.noaa.gov/

Use the NOAA site to find out the latest weather conditions, including current storm watches and warnings that have been posted throughout the United States. Click on "Education Resources" at the bottom of the page to find a number of activities dealing with weather.

A Paleo Perspective on Global Warming
http://www.ngdc.noaa.gov/paleo/globalwarming/home.html

This site contains information about global warming, which is a gradual warming of Earth's atmosphere. Learn why some scientists are concerned about the impact global warming might have on our environment.

Weather Links
http://www.hurricanehunters.com/wx_links.htm

This site focuses on hurricanes, including a history of those that have caused serious damage. You can also click on a link to the National Hurricane Center.

Important Words

air pressure force of gases in the air pushing against something, such as your skin

anemometer instrument that measures wind speed

atmosphere region above Earth's surface that is filled with gases that make up the air

barometer instrument that measures air pressure

humidity amount of moisture in the air

hygrometer instrument that measures humidity

Index

Meet the Author

Salvatore Tocci is a science writer who lives in East Hampton, New York, with his wife, Patti. He was a high school biology and chemistry teacher for almost thirty years. As a teacher, he always encouraged his students to perform experiments to learn about science. When Mr. Tocci is not writing, he spends the summer months sailing. Before he sails, he checks the weather forecast provided by the National Oceanic and Atmospheric Administration (NOAA).